Soil Searching:

Pamphlet on the origin of productive thoughts by means of natural selection of land use, for the preservation of every mind in the ease of life.

Soil Searching

ISBN: 978-1-907540-68-4

First edition published in August 2012
Published in Great Britain
by the Anchor Print Group Ltd

© Andrew Barnett

All rights reserved
The moral right of the author has been asserted.

No part of this book may be reproduced or transmitted in any form or by other means without permission in writing from the author, except by a reviewer who wishes to quote brief passages in connection with a review written for insertion in a magazine, newspaper or broadcast.

For my Dad

'To do what lies within our power to help the developing countries to provide their people with the material opportunities for using their talents, of living a full and happy life and steadily improving their lot.'

Definition of Foreign Aid, from a British Government White Paper on Overseas Development featured in Small is Beautiful, E.F Shumacher

Preface

My English teacher, Ms Pettigrew, taught me a little Latin with Brian Friel's Translations. She once said that I'd be understood yet. She's probably well upset that I've put her at the head of this appalling read. This garbled mess is, reader, for you to understand some of the expanses of thought and landscape that my mind or yours can soar over. I just hope it translates well as I laser ideas onto paper, society and stone with the reckless abandon of a pointed index finger. Encapsulated in this text are several portals that I have stumbled through whilst meditating on good things. In dreaming of doing the world some good; some scientific and other chuckleworthy truths arrived for me.

I was originally going to pen this short book Mien Leichtigkeit, as a send-up to what a potato peeling nazism or any apartheid, including soilism is. I decided against that title for the sake of my skinhead brothers. Rootworms are now also munching through counterfeit crops of the twenty-first century to scupper the plans of soil segregators. You are reading a short musing and I haven't dug too deep into any subject, considering this somewhat of a test-bed next to the expanses of other writers that I have read. True prospecting can be done by you, as you poke through yours and my hidden recesses and neglected walkways. I name-drop for a good reason, I could do some proper droppings but I'm no goat. Every person or business that I have mentioned herein gives you an aperitif of some of the things I've been pleasured to dine on. Hardly Chicken Soup for the Soul, this is more like Chicken Manure for the Mind. Oh so gracefully I love, I farm, I consult; I do not write books! Regularly. For a meatier morsel look at their works whether book, music or entertainment. This is more love than sense and more play than a work-the-land laden treatise. I'm a lover, not a worker, it makes more sense and you get more done with a smile. Those to whom I've referred I respect highly. If this reads like an advert it's supposed to. Buy stuff, especially pamphlets by Andrew Barnett, NOW! Sale On! Only 2 copies left! Hurry! Limited Availability. Terms and Conditions don't apply. NO REFUND! Home again, home again, jiggity jog.

Instead I have chosen to weigh in against my good friend Charles Darwin for a good old punch-up. I'll Rocky IV-Apollo Creed him off a £10 note later via a letter to his lovechild during the Marple Mystery that is, the pamphlet in your hands. I'll share a thought with you. Just the one. It always troubled me that the survival of the fittest animals should be applied to human beings and we should become doings, not even human, as a result. Like Dr Bruce Lipton, Tim Linton or Jean Baptiste Lamarck, I consider life not to be a struggle but more of a relationship between family and friends. Enemies? Yeah right, you gotta love 'em.

I write like I talk, so you are reading the mind of an alien crop circle-dancer. Chants: "I, I, my, my, my, doh, reh, me, me, me, we". Mais oui, please do not expect a neatly clipped argument with moot points. Too much stage-diving, too many crew room chuckles and years, YEARS in Anti-Social Services methinks. I'll cover farming, thinking, Darwinism and love in this text, guess the odd one out. No, there's no research, as I'm too good at maths to wrap myself in a shroud of numbers. Facts is facts, opinions are just that; tell me if anything you are reading is a concrete fact. Forget research for an hour or so and lose all concept of statistics. Research has shown that studies into stuff are infinitesimally finite and that 98.7436948579334433221 18% of statistics do not count. Can you count the air molecules that have just left your lungs? Or state for me now how many atoms are in a glass of water? Ahhh, you missed one.

This is a vehicle for me to take my longings into the tangible realm like a fire engine truck beeping you out of its way, heading for a hydrant to hose down humanity. Shower time. I've sown and harvested, before the reaper scythes anyone. Far be it from me to withhold corn when it's in my hand, cropped and ready for sale. Society appears so meagre to my eyes as it strangles itself with words such as austere, double-dip and re-hypothecation, whatever that means. I am not easily muzzled and it would appear that we need a re-think, a dreamy one… A BIG dreamy one. Men have dreamed, fought and died for me to publish this, so I have this nap you read and it is my short walk to freedom. Freedom is the right of ALL and is the only acceptable standard of living in this sped-up, pent-up time we enter into. You must always feel free to change your mind and this pamphlet is a flood in a drought of happy thoughts. Telling you to let your mind out of the jail cell lodged within it. Freedom comes not with guns and bombs but with ploughshares and humility. How can swathes of thriving saplings be deforested in the blink of an eye or the cropped thing regenerate? Well, if you garden and tend to a good standard, you'll know. What I have written is a short book and a cranny. Row your boat over my compacted clay, fine top soil and patches of pond perpendicular to the wind. All is re-packed as a way to avoid bully beef ration lines in yours and mine own rumination.

The world has written in such a linear fashion for so long that it's become nucleated. Always left to right and never right to left or in a cyclical waltz. To the window, to the wall, please…One, two, three. Allow me to institute this diamond jubilee of dosey-doe conversation. Call it Penbook and I'm Mark Zuckerbarn. You're the apprentice and I'm Lord Barnald Sugar-Trump. You're fired. Or was that me, sacked three times in three years for being a lousy report writer? Figures. I'll dust myself off and carry on then. If you're anything like me, you'll want to learn how to smile sweetly after the poo pies from The Help have been served and ingested. This is my initial public offering and guess who's just pulled one of those geeky know-it-all faces? Time on my hands and my side Magazine is now on sale. It floats my boat to mention that all networks on land and sea are joining up as roads into Roma in a sort of theory about unified fields of the mind and the exterior. These annotations are motorways of the information age autobahnpikes. Fun, fun, fun in a Kraftwerky stroll.

Plenty of billboards coming up along this journey; testament to the fact that I have been marketed to since I was a twinkle in the eye of a little known star. If you have any reservations with what I have written, here is your automated message, "My staff are waiting now to field your conquests in word and inaction. Sorry, in action. Thankyou for waiting until you're pushing up daisies, your all is important to us."

Yes, my comfrey tea-scented thoughts, sweet smelling though they are, are of choosing to beautify the rocky ground of life's crises in the mind first and make a hard place in reality function wonderfully for me and all human doings, sorry sayings. Sorry. Beings. I've forgotten who's right and wrong out in the world today. Of more interest to me than tonguing a judgement call is a rally to both minds and personal spaces, to repair the terraces of the world. In the city, in the field. My ultimate aim in coining this bit is to avoid torrential landslides of mind and body perhaps even soul for the love of money hoarded to your hurt. Stingy miserly thinking can do that; hurt you I mean. So I share this, my only freshwater salmon. Stingy is now defined as Capitalist. Miserly is hereafter known as Communist. Both Capital and Commune are now in bed today like John and Yoko after disagreeing with one another on their cold warmongering (Cap and Commie) honeymoon. All you need is love.

The new world currency is the provision of access to a heart full of agape through a tool, not the brothel of funds. This text is a threshing instrument about to beat to chaff age-old arguments that have stood for centuries. With a tirade of nonsense, you say? There are not too many people on the planet, there are too few. If I hear any more talk of lack of resources, I'm off to farm the tundra to prove there's plenty of unused space and stuff.

This pamphlet is east meets west. Northern hemisphere meets New Zealand. Think of me as a Russian Bear in a Harris Tweed flat cap. Double-barrelled shotgun names draped on every paragraph's elbow crease, breeks, gundog, pheasants on a hook. In spite of the size of my gut and claws, I've shared this delicacy with you. Truth be told, I've ended up living more like my heroes than I care to mention. A Sepp Holzer on his Kramerterhoff showing the regulators just regulation or a Paul Stamets, devising new ways to save the planet with myco-love. Those two men alone have shown me how facile it can be to take a desert from anywhere in the world; a balding pasture or a monocultured pine wasteland, and turn it into mighty fine soil.

True, I come from a family of semi-literate Jamaican farmers, who are the ancestors of slaves from the African continent. I would like to thank Johnny Depp and his shipmates for getting my folks through Kingston's customs on the Jolly Amistad Roger in a true act of Hollywood piracy. Let freedom ring eh? Give us our free! I was born match-fit, ready and free as the wind in London in England. I bop into this scribbling like the newest Flatulentine rap star suffering from seditious over-gold, or dystopian blatheritis. Trouble is, as I said, I'm a free man, no labels hemming my quotes in. I personally am in no competition with the other x=I dunno how many billions or so of inhabitants in this field. I lose hands down to the ripped, rippling muscle-bound brickhouse beefcake; seasoned gaudy gambler or Bentley-driving fatboy quintillionaire. I also thank them for showing me where I can win and for secretly conspiring my wellbeing. I'd like to contribute to theirs and your bandwidth, if we'll only stop yacking about one another and comparing him with her…On highspeed big-mouthed blogspot broadband. I hope you enjoy what I've scribed and if not please pen my downfall. This is not about bettering other books or another person, not even a dead person. This is to put my heart at ease and to set the record straight about my identity next to you. To draw distinction between facts and opinions. To elucidate exactly how I have gone from a capital city dweller where I was born and bred, to a farming consultant in Oo-Aarhickville with proper ideas about how to feed the world. Sorry Mr Geldof, no songs as the goosey is cooked, scoffed and where shall I wander next? I know: To the woods to hang out with Ben Law.

If this makes no sense to you, read on to the end if you can bear it. I believe that there's at least twice as much good stuff as that sad ballad going on in the world today, if someone, anyone, will communicate it. Some of today's shackles: Fake love with a phoney smile, walking into a dead club playing and/or reciting zombie nursery rhymes in order to hypnotise the listener into purchasing tat, or other marketing clowns wearing clown clothes with clown regulations to paint frowns or smiles on society's face. All have this in common, they lack liberty and real loving. Love sits outside of Destruction's train tracks, looking down on its little train-set valley, chuckling, knowing that it's truly beloved and sexy like BLAM! Relationship over religious or nefarious codes for me, where the weak's needs are cared for first, that's true religion.

I once met the London graffiti writer POW! He told me that he was intent on writing the acronym Prisoner of War on some wall, somewhere. I suggested Power of Words instead. Choose them carefully or don't. Now, to separating photons from voids like china in a bull shop. Let's speed light up and drop a mass of ignorant thoughts from a great Hitchcock height. Cleverly, energetically? Einstein!

Fanatics, Infidels and Opportunists, lend me your eyes. Not only am I an incredibly generous fellow but I have devised a read to construct a dream before your very eyes. I am from South West London or maybe East London and every other postcode in the world where young men dream of being kings of their own destiny. I said kings. Queens, you'll agree that being a democratic republican of your own destiny is a kingdom divided against itself and lacks the excitement of regal pleasures of the heart. Let these political football teams of the past come together and have a huddle for earth's sake. They're in it for the money? A prostitute reduces you to a nub of bread.

This incendiary text is written:

Firstly, by a complete fool speaking neither wholly highbrow nor low coarse language with the intention of planting self-fertilising, mat-forming plants on the cracked hematite of the planet. This is televised in 12-dimensional quiff-popping qubital tachyon plasma pulses. Catch up? Stand still whilst this slaps your headback, this is pluperfect. Each word is beamed over the oceans, into the dense plains and across the heavenlies. Like a sperm whale's clicks, there's a kick to them. When you gawp at this media maelstrom you'll see why I paint my image so clumsily. Like Horrid Henry grown up, tanned and ruddy reading a wrap-up of the industrial age. In a cartoon, not a movie. Too busy discussing landscape or husbandry with John Bull to bother with proper production or meticulous editing. We're posturing as men do. Leaning out of our respective souped-up Landies. When we talk like we are now delicacies are being strewn, healing stuff germinates, crops and is chopped up for a tonic before I've truly started the pamphlet. When we've parted ways the crescent of your thoughts is so Ur, fertile, even Father Abraham would say, "That boy done good!" Abe Lincoln will get out of the ground, chuck his top hat up like liberty just graduated. Chairman Mao will come back with a big blue book and rescue the employees contemplating suicide in one of a trillion factories.

Second, with knowledge that there are much greater minds than I waiting in the wings with better punctuation and syntax. The utmost I could possibly achieve would be to contain my imperturbable hope in a mere scrambling of jots and tittles for tweeting your twaddle twain over.

Afford me a third.
This is written for the promotion of peace. Real quietly confident peace. NO werewolf chuckling in a fleece, with latest pear tree product of good and evil in paw. Pear have brought out the Pee-phone, Pee-pad and Pee-pod in quick succession. NO saying stuff is gonna get done when it AIN'T. Let's make yes, yes and no, no. I sit in repose and rest, as I renounce the vampires of ignorance and fear and am quick to chop off their squid-like limbs via good old Parker fountain sword ink and paper. Peruse this Great British Sterling silver garlic-scented stake of a

bullet. Let your oars stir up your own gifts as we meander this river of mind piddles, sorry, puddles or is that pooing...Sorry pooling?

WARNING: There will now be a rude awakening if the world returns to wickedness as usual. I've bought the truth and you are not being sold it, but told it. Farming for the adventurous and gardening for the less so, is one of a myriad of gates to productive thinking and thus a way to loving more than you and your little tribe of uber-bears, bulls, otters...I care not. Get your hands dirty and forget surviving; begin to thrive. Choose to Live, to Love! Overcome just existing.

Get Your Hands Dirty

The best suggestion that I can give is to improve one's mind with a spot of gardening in the outdoors. Says the soil connoisseur savouring the flavour of a fine vintage manure. The self-confessed plant freak jotting this down might have a slight bias and may very well become a worse writer as we go along. Frittering away the hours in town and country for the love of such, doing selfish and selfless simultaneously. It proves good for the mind, keeps you as fit as an Irish band's lead fiddler and adds a level of genuineness to one's inward smile that the Guinness intensifies. Only touch the black stuff if it's as a want to get one's hands dirty, not a need to. Leave it altogether alone if you have an, "If I don't work the land or network the room, the sky will drop" attitude, it's supposed to be good for you, for Pete's sake. Gardening or socialising I mean. Such foreboding could damage one's Chicken Licken-sized cranium, housing the most pickled walnut brain ever created. Ruining the taste of social genius lube in your glass or the hue of gift in your mind. It is to be a retreat, an adored adorned outlet. That noontime reverie in the hammock of life. If not, oh well, perhaps tinkering amongst floral trumpets could sweeten the music of one's thoughts past a monosyllabic autotune.

Gardening, farming, more specifically, improving a space, is somewhat of a gateway gift. Anyone who dares and wins can take off on as many tangents as the human mind can proffer. To the keenest of land and mind tenders, your thoughts become the quiet slickness of an earthworm nestling amongst the delicate layers of live detritus. Such deep rooted convictions fertilising the media you slink through even when rising to the surface to excrete a cast. Like Henry Heinz messing about in a backyard. To some it may be just mud and veg. Therefore, ketchup with the 57 varieties and employment of women at upper echelons as envisaged by Henry the LVII, to discover the power of tomatoes, vinegar and sugar. To dip one's hands beneath the surface is like plunging your trowel into the human psyche to see what encourages, fortifies, beautifies. Ask Barry and Michelle at that ol' White House 'bout that there garden. It is the stepping out into an infinite number of errors with the expectation that things will be pulled up, plucked off, gorged or beheld with pleasure in and out of season. In the making of mistakes one also develops one's own style as unique as a brainwave or ocean wave for that matter. My style is: Clear it, chuck it, tend it every few days or weeks. Blank canvas, lush growth, careful placing amongst the rest. English scholar, is that even a sentence? You could call my approach Big Society, to coin a phrase, if you're not afraid. Like a power-steered Land Rover Defender concept car with an electromagnetically-inducted Rolls Royce engine, tearing up to a mountain top dwelling. It gets there over any terrain. Be Stihl my beating chainsaw.

Soil searching therefore lends itself to bigger subjects such as life, science, economy and relationships. All can be messy, tricky, fraught with peril. All the hypotheses are lighter than Vanity Fair until they are practiced. Through persistence it is possible to discover and maintain a delightful physical, meta-physical and mind space that tantalises the eye and smell, arouses the ear, touch, and taste. A respectable reward for time spent thinking and of course, doing. After a while, like anything, it's more enjoying getting things done than thinking too much about it, ask those productivity guys David Allen, Norman Vincent Peale or Brian Tracy, I'm sure them boys nose, now. Am I reading stupid enough? Good.

It has come to my attention that too much time at the desktop makes one's eyes photosensitive and dull. As if a hard day down the data pits had left the book of the face black with coal tar but the lachrymal glands unstimulated. Outside, amongst trees, birds and plants a convergence descends upon one's senses of whether a day is glorious. Ask any hyper kid if they would rather be out exploring, than rocking in a chair at a desk, back, forth, pneumatic foot tapping. In Britain, more specifically England, the attitude is often one that a cumulus is a physical manifestation of gloom unless it comes with a portable device that connects to it. Each cloud ushers in a sense of bleak indignation and is a harbinger of imminent disaster, DOOM! To the properly landscaped mind, every day is counted as all joy. Ms Sunshine grows the plants, the Rainman calculates the drops, both bringing the buds alive on the bogginess like Rachel De Thame and the Plantfather Don Monty. Cloud cover provides moments for gentle reflection. Carpets of snow keep you indoors organising or out throwing clumps of the white shaggy pile at your mates. One of the many jewels in the United Kingdom's crown land is the splendour of her countryside. The ability one has to scale the heathland like a rugged stag or gracefully doe up a peak and enjoy the dappling of clouds and sun rays amongst the panorama. Yes, the property developer attempts to scab these over, but alas she is undone by the jaw-slackening serenity of not being the centre of it all. She discovers that she shares her world with innumerable plants and things a-buzzing and cooing.

A city such as London or New Yoik has some unfortunate subways of thought that tube along its intestines and could really do with the design skills of Joe Swift. These suggest that to get one's hands dirty is to be frowned upon. Shoo, shoo! Dirty, filthy urchin, away from my whitest of south-east Asian trainers. The truth being that, to live in a completely sterile environment is to hinder the immune system from performing its alien task of maintaining the being. Without mud on your hands how could the prolific beauty of cuttings; little strips and snippets of ideas that will form new plants, be distributed for the wealth of others' lives? Ask Carol Klein. The person with mud under their nails is a sort of blessed creature with rare pearls that can only be entreated with love and an open mind. Make one a cup of tea, ignore the unfortunate wreak. I speak for myself and all other messily tidy folk. I personally suffer from

Attention Deficit Hyperactivity Order, so break out DSM XXX. I also suffer from Autistic Spectrum Order, Oppositional Defiant Order, Seasonal Disaffective Order, Cakeholism, as well as being a Spewsickphobic; that's a person in perpetual fear of being tortured with rubbish music.

Every time a hand is placed in the ground and fingers pinch at the slightest bit of glorious mud, tens of millions of microbes are being introduced to one's body for them to work with, regenerate and improve one's way of life. It's healthier than most muck on the shelves in your supermarket and definitely more nutritious than the lettuce in your burger. I understand from that great lady Clarissa Dickson Wright, that the so-called organic mess in a packet at your local daylight robbery store might only have been organic for three days prior to cropping. It may have received all the relevant noxious chemicals that make food look good, not necessarily taste it…Bon Appetit. What you are reading came about from one's desire to grow not just so-called organic food for my country and the world but worthwhile food with no label of a claim. Worthwhile food means that you eat it and it makes you smarter, happier and calmer. Our family tend to grow or rear our own food or get our family meals from the local British Farms that our family has befriended where possible. Some comes from further afield.

Nobody's common, everyone…EVERYONE's a one-off, unique being. Let's stop lumping people together, let's begin to respect one another. That can start uniformly from food being the bouquet garni in live stock. Play on? Or ride on, Hairy Dieters?

In the First World War soldiers soaked their handkerchiefs in their own urine to fight chlorine's effect on their lungs. Now we add it to food like table salt for preservation and no doubt, for the pickling of ourselves. For the convenience of all-year round potentially organic foodstuff, immigrants are brought in to a country near you. Those nameless workers also receive their own personal treasury of chemicals guaranteed to shorten their lifespan for the convenience of our weekly shop. They rejoice to be paid a pittance and are kept out of town. A rant is stewing in me. Capitalism, also known as effective exploitation of labour, stinks. Homogenised, pasteurised (Yeah, you Louis, Louis), uniform milk stinks, but not a nice stink like goat's cheese. Anarchy stinks! It's so boringly predictable. BORING! Anarchy in the UK? Yeah right. That's a stick of Countrylife Johnny Rotten Butter in my flapjacks. Pootube it, punk. Corruption is landfill, a dunghill, One Poo Hill. The microbial action is a perfect hotbed upon which to plant the future both healthy and relaxing. If, when eating the voluptuous flesh of a tomato, you now want delectable, plump red fruit in place of a watery concoction of Frankendung for aesthetic approval, read on. Breathe air not Oxygenated Nitrogen.

It's Alive!

Any good gardener knows that real soil is not sold at the builder's warehouse, it teems with life unlike the hydroponic space-saving derivative favoured by some cannabis and tulip farmers in the intensively farmed and windowed Netherlands. Real soil contains real plant matter, animal poop, maybe even a farmer's piss. Chemically, these things ought to be so, as any mushroom spawn or bacterial pathogen will advise you. Fungi and bacteria, like most civilised societies, prefer real life in contrast to instant tenuous links sitting in a window for sale in the red light district. That's progress? That's not even the 1960's, when love was free. These tiny little micro things known as the kingdoms of fungi and bacteria are designed to break down the most complicated of big corporation formulae with enzymes more potent than any washing powder detergent. Much like this pamphlet is about to break down what up until now may have seemed a boring subject. This is not an invitation to Thomas Crapper (Poogle it, for toilet humour's sake) in your hanging basket but more of a chance for you to think broadly about what happens in the soil beneath your feet. You're on it, take care of it. Even if you live on a boat, beneath the water is some form of soil with an intimate ecosystem. If set in correct balance this will yield pearls or maybe just pommes de terre. At the very worst you may receive a sense of accomplishment and a can-do attitude. You'll be more sophisticated and perhaps produce a wonderful new way of working out the things around you. Whatever soil (soil being like the mind) you have, it can be made to yield fruit, vegetables or just flowers if you like. All it takes is a willing mind with roots of plans sunk deep into the neurons. Be prepared to mess about and relish doing so. My children will readily exhort the benefits of playtime as would I. Yes, you could learn everything you want from going to college but that rather takes the fun out of the whole process.

Step one: Grab a handful of soil or creative outlets

Step two: What is it? What are they? Squeeze it or them. Is it clingy clay or gritty sandstone? This is your starting point.

Once you know what your soil is made of,

Step three: Get an idea about what you are doing. This may just be a case of buying the right seeds for that soil and broadcasting them over the site or website with water or marketing. This is the real BBC news broadcast, so socks over trousers, waders on, wellies over those, pick and shovel at the ready. We might have to dig deep and fork over assumptive thinking. If you've a mind even similar to mine you'll want to mine further and then give away most of a fine yield. Like Emma Cooper on podcast.

From my late teens I had become accustomed to working like a husky dog. This involved shunting heavy objects across vast distances before stopping for a quick nap to conserve any energy. Boxes across concert stages, trolleys across car parks, pizzas across shop. To begin with this was my gardening style. Life was the scrum down and I was guaranteed to push the opposition back as a good Loose-Head Prop would. Fight the landscape and conquer the thing like Alexander the Great in Suburbia. The square metres slowly became a place of contemplation and subsequently an enjoyable space as well as where my children's daily parties were held. All that changed was perspective, the space stayed the same until my mind was ready to translate ideas to substance with right harmony.

I began gardening properly at my mother's home in East London. I was then a social worker with a penchant for rap music. When I was a boy, I thought like your baggy-trousered boy. The garden looked very much like an overgrown version of the street outside my front door. My concrete Sahara of paving slabs quickly became a retreat from the pressures of life. I began by clearing the brush that had grown up between the slabs whilst listening to lectures by Dr. Noble of the North New Jersey School of Rhyme. A good hearty larf while I disrupted my own personal monosyllable of misery along a street that has no trees to this day. These actions said that it was time for a splash of comeliness and that I was the person to usher it in in that space. I took up the task of heaving the paving slabs to a corner of the garden and relaxing into the glorious sun rays on my shoulders from beneath a wrinkled, muddy, sweaty brow. Everything got pulled up as it was mostly a mass of bramble and pioneering plants. A pit was dug for these unwanted, which I burnt. It felt manly, to get cut by cutting back thorns and prickled by plucked thistles. It felt even moreso to start a pit fire and avoid burning my neighbours' fences. That was as relieving as sipping a pint of water walking through the rasping air of a Death Valley heath. Despite the cuts on my hands and the energy expended, I felt alive in the once industrial (and soon to be greened over) part of the English capital.

During the coming weeks of 2004/5, plots were plotted and plans planned, about what to do with the blank canvas to stop the invasion of the same jungle brush of overgrown mess once more. I designed my first garden with a notepad and a pencil and decided over and over what I would do with each part. At work, on public transport, with my family, with my girlfriend, whilst asleep; it was like I was possessed with creating tangible peace.

I would have a lawn with a roman tiled pathway leading through an archway covered with both winter and summer jasmine. This would lead to a decking area at the back where I had mentally stumped the forty foot sycamore. To the left hand side was a screen of Verbena Bonariensis shading the decking area. As one proceeded up the path there would be a lavender hedge to the right so that as one hung the laundry, your clothes would be brushed with the scent, thus calming you. The hypnotic rhythm of the bees and hoverflies ascending from fresh nectar and descending upon pollination would also provide a nice touch to balmy evenings. Like those at the entrance to the Eden Project in Cornwall which I had recently visited. Flowerbeds were to be dotted about in a random shaped edging and a magnolia tree was to be planted to replace the sycamore. This was all in the mind.

Most evenings and a lot of weekends' worth of precious time was spent setting about crafting this jewel.

All of this got done, bar the decking. In a garden, as with what the mind can yield, action is as important as the planning. Both fall flat without the other. A theory arose in my mind after a lot of reading and watching of Gardener's World. I could blanket the surface of the garden with mustard seeds bought from a local Asian food store and this green manure would suppress all other invasive plants and prepare the sand under the concrete slabs for a lawn. In fact it did much more. It helped me to see in the sea of green seedling heads where the sun shone most (how's that for alliteration?), where was fertile and where needed generations of improvements. It enabled me to improve the quality of the soil bringing worms and creeping life back in. I could now identify and eliminate things which I had not planted adding a new terrain to my thoughts.

When I began messing about in the mud, my ideas were ravaged by my grandmother's imminent death. There's a lot of thinking going on by whoever's putting spade after spade of soil onto the coffin in a cemetery. Or by anyone who watches the body go in and come out an urn. Life usually gets drastically different shortly after. Fortunately, a scented rose grew out of the ashes and dust

I'd chucked. She'd been a keen gardener, I'd never really bothered until now when it became my therapy. So I began to amass my favourite plants but wasn't overly adventurous in my outlook as mum's garden is mum's garden. I let the mustard come up thick and lush before turning the soil over as granddad had taught me at his allotment. He had given me a day's work on a five rod plot whilst he cobbled together a shed as only a carpenter can. The next day I was like a piece of the ply-wood he was using. A lawn was strewn over mater's garden as seed, not as turf. I made a narrow shabby pathway in my thoughts: A trench, building materials and path. In revery and then in that space. Pleased with the effort but apprehensive about planting this, my first lawn, I stood back to examine the progression of a concept. Would it work? There was no sign of anything for ages. Then, a few weekends later my girlfriend at the time, Lizzy, told me that she could see faint waves of emerald on the sides of the path. Gold! The blades were arriving.

Such furious gardening was tempered with shunting the petrol bomb on wheels up, down, left and right around the United Kingdom to see new views and plan the years ahead. Plan we did: Marriage, family, farm. There is no joy quite as complete as watching a lawn of ideas that have been hand-sown knit itself together to such a degree that you can put your feet on it without a cake of mud beneath. In the years ahead I would not have that issue. For the time being, I watched contently as my neighbours acquired a chainsaw and stumped a brooding helicopter tree to a twig just like in my mind. My mother's partner would also give the garden a proper lease of life in the years to come. I left mum's place, taking the equivalent of a black taxi cab driver's examination in gardener knowledge onto my next strip of life. In the space of a year, we, my fairer half and I, had bought a home, got married and started a family. My Hippocampus did not prepare me for the shell-shock to unfold.

After my first proper venture, I sowed another couple of lawns before my girlfriend and I went house hunting. I had bent my knee in a Derbyshire peak, so we bought a treasured little place in Leyton, and I remember being insistent that it had a garden. A space for me to consider what to do next, Bill Mollison or Masonobu Fukuoka fashion. It had some shabby flowerbeds with very dead soil and lousy invasive bushes at the front and back. The front remains virtually the same today but the interior is inlaid with love: It is noted that pure gold always outshines 999 even with a touch of dirt on it. What I did notice were the gems of plain white flowers at the head and tail of the house, Japanese Anemones. Being convinced that I could work this space; over the next five years, every spare moment I could get was spent pouring my time into my all-encompassing hobby. This became very much more for me as it allowed me to think about the growing recession that I could see pacing up my street like an armed man. The 'To Let' signs suggested to me that like in the 80's when I was a little boy, talk would turn once more to where the money tokens went. Money? Who needs it? It's only the answer to everything. Do I like it, no, I'm sick of it. But I'll have some of yours…(checks the bread), thanks. I was Nelson and Napoleon in an outhouse of a garden plotting about how to attack the enemy slug and cabbage white on every side. This allowed me to direct the life of my growing family down a path I had never previously considered, farming. My ancestors farmed, granddad had farmed, I, city boy, can farm too.

The Untrained Eye

For eight years of my life I worked as a Social Worker directly for the British Government and later as a contractor in the East London Colonies. The area is rough terrain for any missionary as you may or may not know. I was not even entitled to carry the title Social Worker. Although I worked with children and families I was not allowed to register with the quango holding the title (cries tremulously into crumpled hat held in hand? OR chuckles with shoulder-shaking delight into Scottish designer country wear?) Anyway, down from the Highlands into the lowlands of genetic determinism.

[Aside - letter to Charles Darwin's illegitimate son, Eugene]

My Dear Eugene Nicks,

Dig deep, mind your feeble mind, alright? Or all sinister? I'm none the wiser. Look ahead, you might fall into or step onto a mine, mine even. That would throw you into the airy cove of a treasure trove that is the ease of life, goony. Like a wet flannel slapping into a full to a brimming well's bucket. Don't you love a mental picture? Pooetry in motion. Oops, poetry.

My head droops. No, Mr Nicks, I never broke the mould, me. Just another one of those silly inferior dark-skinned chaps, says Charlie. My mate: Your father, Mr Darwin - what a character. He's a top fashion designer to this day of the wisecracking variety. I remember him saying only yesterday, "Pink is better than brown you know, check the haute phrenology. Let's have a squabble backstage about which labels to bear. And clump people, sorry, animals together in a fashion line of tick-box seasonal patterns...With flair darling. They can then take these off the rack and have them saunter about according to their melanin content. This one's in black, this one Latino

Cappuccino". He once told me in a library that my dad used to swing from the trees and I was most offended. I told him that it was nonsense to do so and asked him if it was truly enlightened to incessantly pull the race card. He insisted that I wear his argument that I was a bathing ape! I'd rather saunter breezy hillsides in corduroy and tweed thinking of my wife and personal Regina. Would rather tend trees and layers of foliage knowing that my letter to you is no random occurrence.

I mutter as I write, dear 'genie. And sorry if I'm rubbing you up the wrong way. But "Why choose roses over salvias? Uliginosa is like sky on a stem, a waft of Souvenir du Docteur Jamain as the smell of a summer's day". I need more than your three wishes, so I've taken innumerable amounts of candles to my dinner and birthday party. Mud cakes, mud pies, mud salads, mud baths. Whilst we're visualising, I'll have both bits of your spectrum blended into these even-handed panoramic meadows, in spite of my previous instructions to you of a community playing the blues and a separate plush purple one above it. I muse on this mountainside like a master of soil and thoughts, before a short drive into town. One pint of lager-flavoured, chicken and toasted Stilton cheese kebab milkshake with pineapple, lamb, fish paste and ham topping, please. Now to spewing town centre friday night love on Monsieur Darwin's intentional false garments, whoops.

When you get here let me show how I prepare raised beds, the span of ten hectares with unearthly ease. Every day you'll catch me here chuckling as on the cover of my richly crafted pamphlet, with my very stupid gait. My personal catwalk, is here in part, courtesy of your pater's cheery smile. (On the back of a £10 note soon to go out of circulation, reader, it's lovely). I could never quite smile like your dad, me being forced to stagger about in my sobriety. Unlike your papa, I am made to drink vast gulps of freshest tasting, crystal purest, cleanest, naturally filtered, spring water gushing forth from the brooks up here. I'd much rather take his beagle out for a voyage. Of course I'm being sarcastic, 'genie.

AHHHHHHhhhHHHHHHh! I just wiped my mouth and strutted on. My left arm raises my flat cap to my wife and children, revealing it's testosterone-charged muscle-bound slaphead. Never mind, it's truly refreshing to jump in the family chassis of this DC120 electric Landy. Shame your pa thinks I'm not bright enough to drive it. To answer your question on genetically modifying anything or enslaving another precious human? That's as smart as Charlie D;) guffaw, lol, gsoh, l8r, xoxo. Things quite happily modify themselves in my rubbish gardening experience. Frankenpoop chic couture from Champagne Charlie to say otherwise, clearly. Or maybe just another panic attack of froths from his drunkard friend Tom Malthus. It's an awful shame that an ex-man of the cloth was not fruitful enough to multiply good news. I extend my apologies to you if this all reads like a chimp at a typewriter. It must be a completely random occurrence right, with me Hawking your Dawkin, 'genie.

Hoo-hoo! Haa! Haa! Sorry, I'm so uncouth. Chuck some bananas at me. Help me move with the times and embrace that I am a mere robotic animal chasing paper currencies which I love, unable to imagine, capable of succeeding only through the pure bread, sorry bred rice...Sorry race. Being the kind of backward counter that I am has led me to the "delusion", to use your word 'genie, that the human spirit is infinitely larger than its humus shell, pocket wallet or any other outward hydraulic indication suggests. The treasured lining more precious than fine gold, silver, rubies and so on. So here's my guarantee that my arguments will hold peoples of all complexions and tongues together for at least three hundred years, as there is no race but the human one. For your divisive thinking 'genie, there are no borders in the world today. No generational gaps or separations between the lives of males and females, this country, that. All merge in on themselves inside where we are made.

There is only ripening, ripe, and rot. Ask a biology teacher.

People are not stock, Eugene. I'm frowning disdainfully now. Tell the walled street for me, the Hampton family, the Docklands and the mile for squares, it's not hip. Never let a human be chained to a wall or stuck starkers on a seat for sale in a shop window like a shank in a butchers.

There you go Mr Nicks, yours, most other fearful and greed-laden arguments polished off like my glass of fresh water in a plant-infused muse.

As parting gifts to you for the future: Do you not think it amazing the way that there's a flash of light whenever a sperm and egg fuse? My kind of relativity. Is it not wonderful that a human goes through all stages of planetary life: Cellular, plant; and animal life both reptilian and mammalian before emerging from the womb a human? To me it's like the (ahem) Big Bang, creation and evolution all wrapped up in the human body. It takes place not over millions or billions of years, but in nine months! OMG! Yes Eugene, tell your dear papa MC Champagne Charlie D, that there are several billion test cases of this theory walking the planet right now that he can croon a ballad rap to. Thus turning his argument literally outside in, or is that, inside...OUT? Haha!

Yours sincerely,

the Little Chuckle Brother.

Back to the High Road. So, anyway, after pounding the mean streets and receiving cups of tea from many unwelcoming families that had the pleasure of my company, I would come home. Ahh, to water (AHHHHHHHHhhHHHHHHhhhhHHHH!) my postage stamp sized seed of sequoia dream. To see what had changed, if anything, in the past few hours. I turned that A5-sized turf into a floral pampas frontier in my mind first and then into the real thing. Most of my evenings were spent honing a skill. A faculty for observation, patience and optimism that what had been planted on surface or way beneath was worth waiting for. I also ploughed into the ugly considerations of the day, sowing that I was a husbandman right up there with an Alan Titchmarsh or Don Monty Don. A farmer as good as the black one known as the Black Farmer or Jimmy Doherty, the Crackling King. After eight (or maybe 8000) years of report writing, what you read is evidence that I decided to go all-in and write a spaghetti western instead of face-scraping, preening and getting into scratchy office-crimped polyester. Now to a salt marsh.

[Follow-up Aside - Look, Eyeballs, don't complain about me dropping name upon name, business upon business. I have to compete with jiggly-bottomed rap videos, 3d movies, internet and a whole host of other marketing strategies including Barbie whom Pink Floyd sang about. What a pink plastic machine! Either I do this or you leave this paper by the toilet, capiche!?!]

Sprints uphill. The truth could not have been further away from the reality. Successful gardening/farming requires a maturing of one's character. There's no management that rivals the office of the soil I'm told. Once cropped, crushed, matured and mastered thereafter, you can pour the mellow wine into the glass of your life and that of others celebrating with jubilation. Once a gift, any gift, is concrete in your thoughts to the point where, in open earnest, you know what you're doing, there is no recall. Even if, to the untrained eye, it looks like an incomplete and utterly insane pamphlet full of mouth-frothing spittle, you have to persist forwards much like a motorway journey or a ganglion in the mind through hell and high water. To head out into any space with intent is to take your palette in hand and become Van Gogh very literally putting your comforting sunflowers on the surface of a canvas. The painter is never understood until the finished product and is always walking backwards into what the rest of the world walks into. It is to take your beans and chuck them down expecting them to grow to Brobdingnag. Alternatively, the space could become the child-like paintings I once saw in a top gallery that I found both depressing and puerile in the same breath. Some will, some won't. With persistence through failures you develop an understanding of why a human bean (bean signifying a thought) struggles to do so and how this can be overcome. Gardening has shown me that nothing is impossible for the person who says it can happen. I am planning right now to take what I have learnt in dressing other people's farms and gardens (and my own secret place) and apply it to the countryside, and then the world! (laughs like an Audrey II).

Big Garden in Little Body

I had the pleasure of staying at a beautiful cottage in the Leicestershire countryside once. My family enjoyed the two nights spent there, eating at the local restaurant and spending time with relatives. On Sunday morning before we headed off, the farmer who owned the cottage gave me a tour of his an hundred and fifty acres of family fields. In that hour I felt more at home than I have felt in my lifetime in a city. We drove the off-roader with the sheepdog's head nestled on my knee to and fro over sown and pastured fields. To little projects that the farmer had going on. I understood what he was doing and was able to contribute several more ideas to the set-up of wood chip pits planted with willow and the like. I had not grown up in the countryside but my mind was able to burst into life as I was in my element, chiefly a big BIG garden like the one inside of my heart scaled down. We stopped to cut mushrooms that looked like fairy rings to me, and continued on considering parish boundaries and the nature of sheep herding. I was curious to find out how he had maintained such a healthy flock through crises for one. Terraced undulations of a previous generation's effort were visible under our wheels and I decided to create new ones of my own, first in mind and heart, then in mouth and action.

I meditated day and night on the wrong things, such as the painfully uncertain situations in which I wrote all of this. See, it even ruined the flow of my words! Debts looming like snail shells stuck to wall, dreams still longed for in a web of confusion, life not regal enough on the recliner. Backwards meditation is worry. I was therefore eager to carve out my own path as unique you or I. I mused on the past glories of hiked Snowdonian hills, beach walks in Cape Wrath and Fowey, or of sneaking underage beers or very special old pale into gullet in La Rochelle, L'ile D'Oleron and Cognac. My thoughts glided back down black slopes as I Roni Sized up the ski resort of Andalo in the Dolemites in the dew of my youth. It's now like I've gone full cycle to those blurry smoke-filled years and can no longer string a sentence together. My mate Dave said, "You don't drive through the rear view mirror".

We, my wife and I, began to discuss where to head off to as headquarters for the family. She had been chasing a similar dream all across Europe. In spite of all of our wrangling rambling, I was later to discover that we had only re-discovered the track our respective families had previously run on as the baton was handed to us. Her maiden name and that of her mother's gave suggestion of some field work with flocks. My granddad had taught me how to plant and crop beans, like he had done since he was a boy. My wife had grown up on a farm, selective about which milk she drank and playing in the fields with her sisters. As a little boy, I had secret hideaways to get away from the girls at home in Pollards Hill. To get tadpoles with my friends and spy on the estates below before a game of jumper goalpost football or a roll down the hillside. As a young man, I had sat on the hills and commons in South and East London and contemplated my piece of this life whilst eyeing the thousands upon thousands of homes in that part of the world.

We settled for the captivating spleandour of Middle England. As this seemed the best base to explore a childhood longing. Discussing farming fare takes me back to being a child in wonder. Having spoken with farmers young and old, I've had the temerity to consider new ways to approach the same old adage: The production of life-giving delicacies for consumption. Funny old thing life and how what you dream of whilst even five seconds younger can manifest itself. I guess it boils down to how you lay down the tarmac on the red carpet. How quickly you can get the knack of doing so. That's proper forward meditation.

A garden, a farm, a space station or a thought should be laid out as a literal one-off; a gilded masterpiece although nothing new is being done. Check the Royal Horticultural Society's Flower Shows as a good start. The Chelsea Physic Garden's pretty good too. They work wonders with garden space there. I admire the fecundity of their concepts. Space exploration and colonisation can be translated to any size or dimensions; up, down, bigger, smaller. The sound engineer and general genius Bob Mossey, taught me that in one word: "Scale". This is rather fetching to me considering Blighty has no exploration of deep outer space due soon in its name. Other than space cadets such as yours truly grabbing galaxies of soil to encourage naturally grown caring for the planet and the master race. That being humans as I have aforementioned.

There must be no imitations but something original crafted with reverence and wonder, like a human thought or fingerprint. Gardens and more importantly, the mind should not be a mere pea gravel coffin but life should be incorporated in, or it will eventually grow through, around and even over, masking the original expression. Ask those zen garden blokes in Japan. One need only look at the nightmare sitting on the world's doorsteps. This is nothing to do with poverty in monetary terms but more to do with a lack of concern for one's body and that of others. These walking cities of cells or electrons that we are. A general ignorance to the fact that one's hands and heart can create a thing of beauty. Have a heart, plant a flower and pretty up grim cityscapes, much like a smile brightens the face and happy thoughts cheer the body. I have seen upper level flats (condos) in and around the world that have used a Crysanthemum or Pelargonium in a flower pot to brighten sombre surroundings. The complexity of any array of floral joy is as deep as the soil holding it. This can vary from a few layers of plant and animal detritus to millennia of ecological forming such as mountains, watersheds and volcanoes. The great thinker will simplify the most complex of landscapes and transport the alluvial silt down like a river into the sea of awaiting bodies. They'll also have the common sense to lock up a portion meet for their own consumption back close to where the water was shed in drip-drop fashion. Access granted over insight hoarded, patent pending, terms and conditions apply, copyrighted, trademarked and all other padlocks.

As my favourite comedians, the Goons, used to say, "It's all in the mind". If one thinks that a space can be lush and rich in a matter of weeks, this is possible. It is drastic and may require some realisation of what the space and person can do but it's possible. A can do attitude can, a can't do attitude can't, to paraphrase Henry Ford. It is also of the highest importance that one considers that being smart today is as important as being tough has been to men since the beginning of males. Working smart saves both muscle, brain, and wallet power. But working is not loving. Loving supersedes the given tests and brims over with confidence that all are satisfied with the end result; no text votes, no judges, no visible critics. No direction except outward and therefore no agenda other than to fill the void, no sweat needed.

A practical example, if I may, of what I have just discussed. Pick one of the three.

A garden (or planet) needs to be cleared of rubbish (points of view or dowdy plant corporations) and replanted with 20000 plants in a month, the soil is also incredibly hard.

a) Do nothing, kick yourself, lose hair and sleep from the stress of an unfulfilled dream (as a painter like Adolf). Start slapping yourself (and your chosen scapegoated race) in the face every morning as encouragement that that feels better than what you've just done.

b) Get ready for hard work (like most hard workers), drink coffee until your heart explodes, get no sleep and spend every moment of the forseeable future digging, net-surfing and ordering, ripping and forcing plants in and out of the ground. Days are now 29 hours long. Weeks 55 days long. You also smell and look a wreck. Prize fighter? You're ER, ICU, A&E. Water frenetically and panic over whether anything worked. Then re-do all of the above. Daily…Then hourly.

c) Buy two million mustard seeds for a reasonable price, throw them on the ground and water them like a lover. Within days of relaxing, planning and restful sleep, decide which plants need to be disposed of and where the 20000 or 20000000 (it doesn't matter, more zeros, less) new plants are going. Video call, text and call close friends and relatives over for a gardening party. They now help to plant by the thousand in rhythm to the music, whilst enjoying good food. It's not strenuous for them as the hard work of breaking up the soil has been done by the humble mustard seed. The barbecue is in full flame. Therefore the job is done enjoyably with style and ease. The rain waters your plot so you don't have to. Flowers bloom, pollinators and general creeping lifestyles settle in. Peace of mind and piece of beauty. Go and sit with a loved one.

My rule for gardening is put a lot of effort in at the start and then take it easy. Your farming day should be short, sweet and thoughtful, because the capillary and rotational systems of your stock, balance the nitrates. If you want to do more, then do so. Please let it always be choice over chore. Silky blooms in a meadow over you bawling, sodden in clods of, is that mud?

Sweet Rhythm or Cacophony?

If tending is not pleasurable what often happens is that one develops the kind of rambling rose that pricks you into more work than rest like novels by Wilkie Collins. The more the words the less the meaning I'm told. The cloud (internet) to me is a crunchy mp3 four track song as opposed to the orchestra playing Vivaldi that is heard when I garden or farm. It's like physical reggae. Dear musicians, layer rhythms with leafy fauna like Stevie Wonder and bejewel them with soft flora like Ian Dury. I do so regularly and languish in each nanosecond of time spent in the open air. So many emotions and contrived situations force themselves in upon one's thoughts, it's good to shake them off with a garden fork and think 4D or more for a change. Much like love, surely there's more to it than some sugary sweet coating on a pop song. Look past a nursery rhyme coaxing a quick flower bedding on a mid-February evening or three bags full. We are, or rather I am as a man, required by society, high and low, to act like a super fly. Instead I would rather send said insect vector across my fields carrying mushroom spores that I placed on its feet to clothe the dirt (no disrespect to creeps). We bat away the very things that can help us provide food for others as we consider them harmful to our health.

There is (or was) an entire industry built on the fear of superbugs killing your child in cold blood. Truth is, most mushrooms that we eat, find bacteria such as those killer superbugs tasty beyond belief. Therefore grow Shiitake in hospitals, restoring health to the patient whilst destroying pathogens. World peace is impossible if we insist on destroying or homogenising the little things with inorganic crop sprays and pasteurised milk. Small creatures should give us serenity in uncertainty that they are so resilient. They, like Audrey Hepburn, provide the apostrophe and space to make world peace read, "I'm possible". Or are we the pests that we claim spoil the crops? Why not apply pesticides to ourselves? We are? Shocking! With a botox smile. Life is so brief, that we should mess around outside a bit more instead of limiting ourselves to a building and a screen or trying to be what we're not. Develop your hobby and let it photosynthesise fresh air whilst you muse on it in your backyard, field or local outdoor space. To do so is to embellish the whole planet rather than just tag a wall with your street name like a person that pisseth on a wall.

Thoughts, songs and ideas replicate and manifest themselves in and outwardly. They can be guns and bombs to solve the fear of guns and bombs or poppies to beautify a dead space. Garbage, garage or grime in your mind is the same thing in your walled garden, stupid girl. Rot it down, park a car in it, plant in it or something. Alternatively, expect an abundance of carrion from flies and cockroaches to culture vultures ruining your movie set. You'd want to step on a King Tubbys dub for why?

It is fair to say that stock prices in girls, guns and ganja rhetoric have peaked and triple pig slop troughed, by the hairs on my chinny. Rap music like society indicates that street slang, freedom of speech and thought have been invaded by a bunch of skid-row slaves with exorbitant funds on a hegemonic ego, power and acid trip. When paupers rule, the world is full of pill-popping, grasship-hoppers ready to jump into a new cast iron frying pan of their own smelting. Sending evil report to all and sundry…What's good? Some slaver with no Flava becomes God and you're a sacrificial zealot? Come on, or rather, come off it: The crack-cocaine I mean; and the selling of musical ice to kids, life is more than hits from a pipe. I admire the capacity to say what you feel, especially when it frees minds like Public Enemy in 1987 or today. In the multiplicity of words there is the potential for fetters to be distributed or disbanded. Enough already with the incessant doom and gloom broadcast puking through every orifice like the wheels on the bus.

Live life enough to know that death's picking and chewing of the carcass is quite tedious, not a scary subject. It is easily crushed between thumb and index finger with a tissue. Life with no passion is SPOOKY. It's like a black t-shirted talent judge from nowhere critiquing all music as to what should be in your ear. Your ear. Dig down into your thoughts or the soil, things are going on there. To me, soil is a place of germination where googolplexes of new things are fed and grow at the same time. To me, the mind is a place where what your hands will do germinates from. The actress Ruth Jones described death as something that makes you want more of life and I'm inclined to agree. I once sat down with a man in his eighties or nineties who looked like he was knocking on Heaven's door, in a woodland in the Devonshire countryside. I asked him about his passion which was sailing and discussed mine, take a guess. He believed that more people should garden today to get an accurate pace of life. We then both took a fleeting tree-top zip-wire to our destination at the foot of some pines. I never saw him again after that weekend.

Recapping, death can be a fearful thought that is a kind of leach that sucks real life away from you. I can sit and ponder the one-off meetings eternally or I can let the spirit of a unique encounter impact my today, my now. The rank amateur sees life or soil as a flat, dead, mucky substance; it is anything but. Exploration and reflection on soil quality by the least observant shows insects, microbes, fungi, plant roots, even mammals and reptiles. Birds flying above, eyeing it up for a worm. All of which are living and thus moving, albeit slowly, and adapting in spite of the odd carcass. Call it an ecosystem, I call it a relationship. No striving or stressing like the young Charlie Darwin, just life, glorious life.

Go Soil Association, It's Your Birthday

Some like to crowd out land with obsessive thoughts, others like it bare and plain. Both are alike if not done with a modicum of love. A full farm is brimming with triviality and a barren garden void of wisdom if the space is not occupied with a warm dexterous hand. The crowded garden will become an unsearchable jungle requiring too much tending and the plot of slack lack will have untwined matted thorns and brambles, all for the lack of an attentive eye. Any space is a terrible torment if the occupier lacks a purpose to what they're doing. It is a natural instinct to flit from one job to the other in a space, but if any task is to be successful; one must be like a prevailing wind, travelling from here to there. So when you ply the soil keep one thought in mind, mine is love. The world's oldest profession is not lying back and thinking of England, it is to be a source and sustainer or a tender and propagator of life.

Love, lovey, extinguishes anything but itself, c'est la vie. It's not herbicide, or insecticide and it's definitely not pesticide. Consider, for the sake of a crop one can remove all trace of life from the soil, literally napalming the site clean. Would you not expect it to come rushing back in, life I mean, from every side into its rightful space? Posing a real threat to the next batch of, I don't know (it ain't food) what. Snails jetting in in leather shells like Hells Angels and Cabbage White Butterflies dropping eggs like fighter pilots on your Marxist commodities. Is it a happy occasion to put increasingly crazy chemicals in the bloodstreams of our children because of stony ground supermarket monotone mad mindspace? Death, which is pretty much all the same; pine box, worms, begets itself and negativity breeds more of the same, inwardly in the storm of thoughts, outwardly, shake it all aboutwardly. Turn around, love understands that the exterminated creeping thing is the same pest that sustained our lives up until now. Husky toned Barry White-sang Lurve knows the blight and pest will come back stronger in order to balance itself if needs be. So it coaxes it to rest its disease in a sultry hip-swing of harmony.

When you change a space embrace the fear of unknown quantities. Whatever you find is there for a reason and has a purpose, weevil or hoverfly. When I garden I make so many mistakes you'd think I was on a Rich Dad Coaching course, failing early and responsibly to overcome acronyms of fear. Maybe that just false evidence appearing real. Fortunately for me I make no record of the mistakes I make with trowel in hand but retain what's useful. That way, excess watery thoughts drain off my brain in a Holzer-esque terraced fashion without creating a landslide, or worse a manslide. If I were to catalogue my gardening convictions, the faux pas after faux pas would make me look like a garden Kray brother opening an East End seedy seed club or agricultural Al Capone procuring a bathtub of wine. It is obvious in hindsight that what I do is often more chaff than gold, but nuggets is nuggets.

Instead of beating myself with a large pointy stick for not following the strict observance of legalistic garden sanctity, I like to spread-eagle in the middle between that and hedonistic pap. This allows me to do and get what I blooming well want: Liberty blooming. In so doing I think for myself, and lose the rigidity of both trains of thought, one can then act on initiative like conversation. Flexibility and liquid thoughts are necessary outdoors, that's what you carry inside with you, into your living space, your bed! Into your home or your introspection. Any gardener worth their weight in manure knows that one day or year's weather does not determine the next, so it's nice to hang loose. It is more important to see the cycles of weeks, years and prepare if you can in tens or twenties, perhaps even centuries for the bold. Some top hints to this are the temperature and direction of the wind, moisture in the air, the choppiness of the sea. There are plenty of others waiting to be re-discovered. Whatever the weather, I believe nothing should spur you on to fight your space. If it requires vigour, employ it. Change that space as easily as you change your mind but bring harmony in and rest thereafter. I suggest that a constant fight in a space as beautiful as earth is evidence of some inner turmoil and a lack of Edison lightbulb experiments in a home or in a country. Call it a War on Plants that you quite like the scruffy look of and are useful in their place. After a while you'd think why fight it, think it through and address it inwardly before you set about work, all in your heart and mind. If a plant or tree is dying, let it die, unless you are prepared to find out how to revive it and the plant is willing to live. Its death may result in plenty more life and at the very least feed a whole host of fruiting foodstuff.

When you have a prevalence of an insect, disease, plant or blight do not eradicate it, it is a clue to the solution in thought or mud. Observe and feed the area, as well as applying a natural soil cleanser like garlic boiled in water and cooled down, ready for addition to your watering can. A good book or saying can refresh your thoughts like garlic's effects on the vampire within partying it up. The shock to the immune system will get the sluggard in you or your garden working in your favour. Encourage natural predators and a proper ecosystem. Perhaps a relationship if you can handle it. Healthy vegetables can be grown in any space even when it is teeming with a plethora of space invaders, plant munchers and root ruiners.

Healthy lifestyles can be grown in any space even when it is teeming with a swathe of burglars, robbers and other assorted takers, see what I'm doing here? Self-seeding monocultures such as nettles and clump-forming plants indicate an abundant chemical element or food source. This is what scientists and investment bankers are hungry for, to dig them out of their quandary. Dig deep, you are reading your solution, so pay for it guys; no naked shorting, exchange traded derivatives or honorary doctorates before you cough up. No chaining my relatives to your wall on that street. To Market, TO MARKET! TO BUY A PLUM BUN!

A patch of nettles, like a patch of entrepreneurs means a lot of nitrogen or silicon chips or another useful element in the landscape, like software boffs in Shoreditch or The Valley. My attitude is one must always overcompensate the minus of too much of something with the positive of access to all, whether concept, knowledge or element from the Periodic Table even. Maybe, say, set up a local wi-fi collective perhaps to pool local resources. That's commonwealth talk. Another way to say that, is to chop a swathe of nettles up to make liquid feed for the other plants and a cup of tea to relieve hayfever. This provides free space, positive visual and physical energy, plus a good crop for all. It stops excessive hoarding by the capitalist cockroach and is not by any means Marxist. Mr Biens Immobiliers understands this as the turning of a liability property's sting into a medicine and a plant tonic; a house of multiple occupants. One can also do the same with painful situations or horrible memories.

Cover the rough patch, any rough patch over with a piece of cardboard and a bit of straw called positive other side-of-the-coin thinking. Never mind. These things happen. Help someone else go through theirs. This encourages worms, ants or different thought trails; the true gardeners of the world, to convert the remaining stems to soil once more under a wet blanket of pulp. Before you know it your joy is cloying. Slugs become useful and provide help converting compressed wood to soil instead of munching your favourite Aeonium. One must encourage even the snail and slug to be productive towards one's endeavours and constantly introduce new concepts to furnish and decorate the old working methods. No death pellets and yes a new idea under the sun. Some old methods will remain as always, others won't. Too much chopping and changing however, shows a lack of direction. Still, be liquid concrete.

Is what I've said in this pamphlet making no sense to you? Oh well, here's a bunch of solutions to some of your societal woes at the time I write this. Here you go in baby talk. Go from the ridiculous to the sublime to get solutions. The answer is somewhere therein. Too much of a resource? Share. Problem? Unhappy? Replace with happy and healthy thoughts. Crisis? What crisis? Allergies? More gingko trees planted, more raw milk mixed with Aloe Vera tforhe children. High crime, low jobs? High grassroots entrepreneurial drive, good food in schools and homes. Wage inequality between the sexes? Men with integrity into the driving seats and women (including the incredibly beautiful black ones that have been hated on for centuries) into positions where they are not subject to saggin' backwards and jock-slapping. They can then educate the boys who claim to be men and the men who would have all men be boys. Miserable place to live? Be a shard of light. Mad Max landscape and economy pending? Top land consultant with ideas that will last down the generations, not another blinking economist going "I think…So, maybe".

Another paragraph of solutions in Gentleman Goo-Goo. Chief Big-Wig inspection of your cub scout tent? Be prepared. No panicking, lots of laughter and self-examination… Rectification and recalibration needed without sluggishness. Milk market rigged to ruin your family-run dairy? Go back to raw milk sold locally and ensure family farm produces an excess of fruit, meat and veg to eat and barter with. Get buffaloes if needed, for top quality society-strengthening milk. Set up a milkman system with electric cars delivering from farm to a base in town. This improves the standard of livestock and milk quality. It also prepares for a future transport industry. Nightmare children to parent? Take your hand off the controls, allow them to govern themselves; thus loving them on purpose as Danny Silk says. You then have more time for freedom, romance. Shoot, happiness. Abject poverty killing your landscape as people poo in your water supply? Plant trees along the stream, both fruit and pollutant-clearing. You'll get filtration, food and as the trees transpire, there'll be more clean rain heading for that place. Kid hooked on drugs? That's the symptom, what's the root cause? Your stinking thinking, the neighbourhood, too much pressure to do well? Unresolved abuse or neglect? Come on! Be honest with yourself first! Livestock or crops being blighted by weather?Terrace the land, place boulders into pond suntraps to passively store heat and release it slowly. That's slower flowing water downhill and climate change in your favour. Ask Sepp Holzer, or ask me. Schmallenberg virus wrecking your lamb? Plant hedges or areas of healing herbs that midges hate and that attract birds and spiders to eat them. The same spaces also have a hoverfly effect. The hoverfly being so territorial, will not tolerate any mere midge in its space. Your cattle all lumpy from Tuberculosis treats from the badgers? No culling. Improve the landscape with a pharmacy of plants for the animals so that they can self- medicate. A few choice herbs here, a few magic mushrooms there; they'll be having a festival called Cowstock. Healthy land, healthy animals, healthy food, healthy me, healthy you. Yes? YES!!! (Punches air, knocking wind out)

Worms and one-footed molluscs create healthy soil and have the quality that I would describe as knitting. Their slimy mucus makes my soil spongy and able to retain more water. More knitters in a space is a factory for me without children in cheaper labour zones suffering. Many fungi also have this quality, running a sort of motorway or 3d internet access across any landscape in order to ferry nutrients to relevant places to produce mushrooms for example. Their spores are like the cloud and their connections on the ground put the hardened gang member's networking to shame. I recruit plants, insects, general nature and therefore I have more employees than all of the rich folk on the planet combined. My employees never ask for a raise or complain about the working conditions and I have thus freed every other person from the shackles of my limited frame of thought. What you have seen or conceived in the the mind as possible often plays itself out in your thoughts tangibly around you. Moreover, what you learn from gardening can invigorate your thoughts. I've learnt the principle of taking wet sand or grit and even just a glass of water and propagating several plants over and over infinitely with quantitative ease that Sir Mervyn King would admire. This helps a shop-bought leek or spring onion give me a meal. Then, bam! A second beckons when the end which has been cut off is sown. Roots are coaxed out from the stub with water and then you put it in the ground. This process can go on indefinitely, is not counterfeiting and is how proper interest rates should work.

Discover the deep joys of making your own natural fertilisers from nearby plants to ensure plant growth forever. Brew your own fertilising ideas for that delectable odour that ranks higher on the wreak scale than a city sewer. Oh, life from a deathly smell, the scent of love. Such is my love for doing so that I am currently working on my own concoction of an all-in-one fertiliser. Firstly to deal with my own crops and then on other farms in the future. This will be used by the sensible gardener as an alternative to the chemical warfare being fought on many an allotment. It is completely organic, of course, in word and in deed and a completely secret recipe. Feel free to invest in your own societal feeds. Steve Jobsy has, and look what the dude propagated!

Apples, whoa dude! Jamie O's always knocking them up in his kitchen. As is Duff, that Charm City Cakes guy. Delicious food, whack the heat up, time for sponge, let them eat! When you operate in a gift it's bound to happen (creativity I mean) and as I said, gardening is a gateway gift. Steer clear of it kids! It leads to harder, faster and more brightly coloured dreams.

It's All in the Mind, Planter

I have listened to savants talk about how they learn a language quickly or get a bigger slice of pie from pi. I've also had the pleasure of living with autistic children in my family as they have created sprawling landscapes on computer systems and we've gawped at the autobots versus the deceptions, sorry decepticons. From their sometimes disinterested way of being, I have learnt that we all have an inner landscape that is now translating itself. The degree of intimacy one can have with it fascinates and unnerves us but it is certainly no spectrum disorder, to look inwardly before living out. It's order at a scale we can barely fathom. But everything in your living space is there for a reason, part of you. Now's a good time, if you're hyper, to get a spade and do mum's garden. Before you become a practice case and get prescribed speed, sorry methamphetamine, in a new chewy, child-friendly orange flavour from your local family doctor. Ummmmm, sleep-slapping happy.

Tell me, how does a man with no job and no money tokens go from gardening at his mum's house, to padding about a farm as a stately ruler? Expanding a thought with dynamic effect and a quick glance in the rear view. Space improvement is mind expanding: My chosen all-terrain ride to glory. Nippy for shifting gears and changing lanes and yet subtle and stationary. The funny thing is that as I've gardened and farmed, I've gone from the rigidity of formulae telling me "plant in this month, crop here", to a simple whim based on observation and visualisation. I took the small potted plants I had in my mother's sunny garden to my dingy shady hidey-hole of a garden. Tipped them out and planted them into larger containers which were like mini-acreages in my mind. The larger containers that had contained fruit trees were planted in a custom-made planter made out of railway sleepers amongst a jumble of plants. I then had room to rip up more paving slabs and plant the first of my meadows. This space became more organised by the day into plants that liked one another's company. I re-filled the fruit trees' containers with new larger landscapes. Now each of the larger containers is not just a mere pot but a separate climate: One sandy and dry, one a bog, another woodland, another pine forest, another land in transition, one a flower garden, another just in the brain. Now in the soil, first in the mind. I pulled up all the slabs in a fit of energy and dissatisfaction with Status Quo rocking all over the world. I replaced the squared stones with a meadow, in the mind, then in the soil to repeat to myself that anything could be done and repaired better than before. A dream, then a reality. Bits and bobs, then a blueprint. Blueprint from architect to foreman and manifestation of such, todah!

The wonderful L-shaped planter that I had made at the back of my garden is a reminder to myself that I will take whatever lot is given to me in life, improve it and multiply it to more than I could personally use. I'll share it with the whole world. Try it, it's fun. No greediness or any hint of selfishness but a way of kerbing a craving for power over circumstance. When you give without the showiness, life is too good. To throw seeds on the ground it is to be generous to the soil, as good thoughts enrich and invest in the soul. By the way, what a generous, thoughtful reader you are. Smile in the mirror, inwardly then outwardly for delving so deep into my mind.

In times when I hear of crisis and lack; gardening, farming or thinking rightly is to have too much in life, rather than too little in Malthusian meagreness or Darwinian strife. Of course you are free to do with your own plot of land and your mind as you so wish. Free to grow Papaver Somniferum in your moody Marxist malady en masse. This writing is invested into the marketplace; a witty invention substituting this fellow at the 2d screen of choppy-waved trades or strolling the street the Desperate Housewives live on. Here I am swooping over meadows refusing to sell my chiselled flabs to wage or appreciation bondage. Terrible affliction to be cheap sex masquerading as peace and love; a succulent strawberry truffle with a horse manure ganache. And a life? It's become somewhat of a stylised advertisement. Cogito I have here the decoding of a mystery. Ergo I do not feel out of sorts scribing this. I mean if you love to do something, put the hours in and then it's not work. It's love and it works real swell. Become it, if the sum of it is worthwhile. A Joshua for whom the Bell of celerity, I said celerity, tolls. That being a lead violinist, with the conductor organising your back-up and the audience oohing, ahhing. You just curl the notes ingrained on your heart.

That fine raised bed with its preceding meadow, was built for me by two unassuming chaps and filled with my daily musings. It reminds me to jot down that from 2004 onwards what I had went up from a paltry layer of soil at the bottom to a part aesthetic, part functional space with flowers, vegetables, climbers providing windbreak hedges, fruit trees and a herb garden. Yadda, yadda, yadda. Like my next adventure, it is part terrace and part experiment. Blah, blather, blah. Instead of the soil being put down and the plants being put into it, the plants are in and soil is added at intervals. The soil keeps being added to the top in the form of emptied out teabags, rotted horse and chicken manure, straw and clumps of soil, cardboard, bricks and stone to passively store heat. Much like problems are heaped on the mind on a daily basis. As I go along I allow the plants to make their way through this and encourage what I want to survive by using an index finger or a Burton Overy dibber to create a perimeter around them. The project has expanded from the back to encapsulate the whole garden and is now manifesting itself into something that would do Sarah Raven proud. It's meadows with too much dinner in it for one family, or one town to eat. Gotta share it.

Just think, a little more than a year ago, I was laid off for the third time in three years…On Friday 13th!!! I now look forward to every batch of supposed bad news, they're solution seeds ready for planting. I also consider the next logical step for someone as keen to garden as I am to be farming. To expand these ideas to surplus; extending an index finger to point during consultations to the intrigued land or society scaper; sharing the wreak of my liquid ideas whilst caring for larger spaces of this planet. Not the moon and not Mars just yet.

There is my brief translation of word to action, love indeed. Love is messy with so much intricate beauty. I have written this for you before I lose the plot and do the stupid things I've already done. And got bored of, mind. Like getting evicted from the Leyton Allotment Association for untidiness three years after I was evicted, by letter. Thanks to you LAA guys, you were amongst my first critics. I love you guys. Thank you so much! I'll tell you about that another time.

To purchase more copies please contact: Thecloudlining@rocketmail.com,

Price £28.99